ELEVATING
wisdom
on the *walk*

COMPANION GUIDE

deepening the walk

compiled by **lori l. dixon** Ed.S.

featuring

NIKI BANNING • CRYSTAL DUNCAN-HOGUE
FRANCISCA ETUOKWU-BENYEOGOR
MANTEQUILLA GREEN • TINA JACOBSON
NATALIE MERRILL

Book design by Callie Revell, callierevell.com

Published by LLD Legacy Publishing, LLC

Printed in the United States of America

contents

dear Reader...

Thank you for choosing to read and dive deep into scripture and your life.

This book and companion guide have been created with you in mind. When the Lord asked us to name this book in the WoW series, ELEVATING the Wisdom on the Walk, we realized it was about going deeper into the stories to heal the pain, trauma, disappointments, realizations, missteps, and even the times we may have walked away from Him. His love, grace, and His Word call us back to walk WITH Him and hear His words in our life.

This companion guide is meant to be used for just that—ELEVATING your walk with the Lord. Whether you do the reflections, scripture mapping, and journaling alone, with a
bible study, or even a group of friends, you will deepen your walk with Him.

Will you join us?

Will you accept the assignment to elevate?

We can't wait to hear! Please join us in our Facebook group, Wisdom on the Walk Author Community. You will find like-minded Christian women seeking and worshipping the Lord.

We hope to see you there! If you decide to write your story with us, please feel free to reach out and we will set up a time to chat. Email me directly at: lori@walkwithlori.com.

Be blessed, Be Bold, Be YOU!

 Lori

walking in legacy

Lori L. Dixon, Ed.S.

Reflection

Where do you believe your legacy in life lies? How will you nurture and grow in it so you are growing IN Him?

_____

_____

_____

_____

_____

_____

_____

_____

_____

_____

_____

_____

_____

_____

_____

_____

_____

_____

The journey of faith is a narrow road. How is that evident in your own life and how would you describe your path?

_____

_____

_____

_____

_____

_____

_____

_____

_____

_____

_____

_____

_____

_____

_____

_____

_____

_____

_____

Where do you need to shift from lack and loss to legacy and love? Identity those areas that may even be deeply embedded within you.

_____

_____

_____

_____

_____

_____

_____

_____

_____

_____

_____

_____

_____

_____

_____

_____

_____

_____

_____

_____

_____

deepening your walk

Scripture Verse

"And now, because we are united in Christ, we both have equal and direct access in the realm of the Holy Spirit to come before the Father. So, you are not foreigners or guests, but rather you are the children of the city of the holy ones, with all the rights as family members of the household of God. You are rising like the perfectly fitted stones of the temple and your lives have been built up together upon the foundation laid by the apostles and prophets, and best of all, you are connected to the Head Cornerstone of the building, the Anointed One, Jesus Christ himself."

Ephesians 2:18-20 (TPT)

Translations

Key Words

Context

Interpret

Application

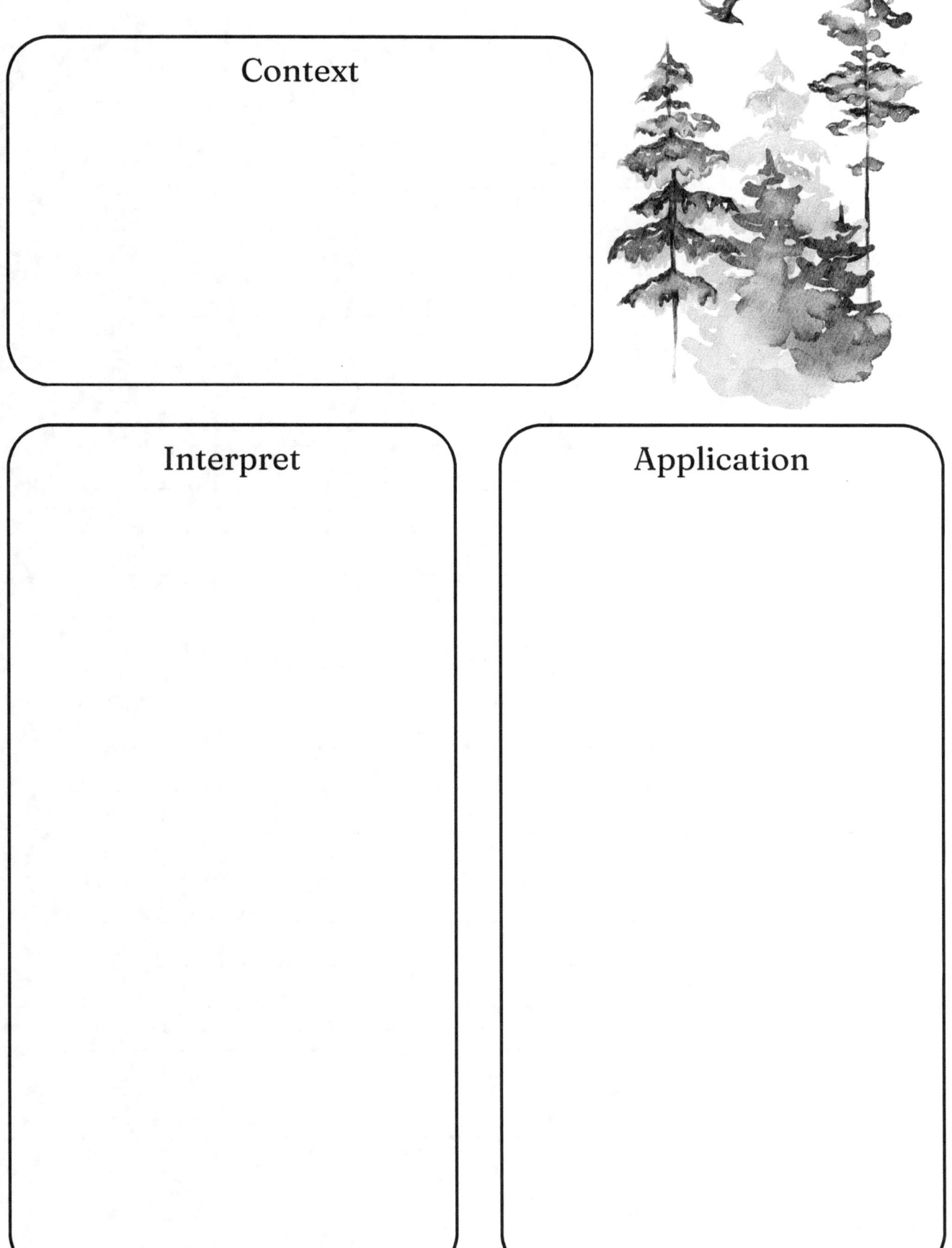

steadfast

Niki Banning

Reflection

Words and actions can hurt. Can you recall a time when you were hurt deeply by someone's words or actions? What did you do with that pain?

_____

_____

_____

_____

_____

_____

_____

_____

_____

_____

_____

_____

_____

_____

_____

_____

_____

_____

_____

_____

Decisions in life can keep us aligned with God's heart for us or take us off-track. Have you ever made a choice that took you away from Him? How did you find your way back?

_____

_____

_____

_____

_____

_____

_____

_____

_____

_____

_____

_____

_____

_____

_____

_____

_____

_____

_____

_____

_____

Life can catch us up in the whirlwind of experiences around us, and it's easy to forget that God is not in the chaos. He is our God of peace, details, intentional love, and steadfast hope. Where have you seen God's steadfast love in your life? What transformation has His steadfastness brought to you?

_____

_____

_____

_____

_____

_____

_____

_____

_____

_____

_____

_____

_____

_____

_____

_____

_____

_____

_____

_____

deepening your walk

Scripture Verse

"Yet the Lord longs to be gracious to you; therefore he will rise up to show you compassion. For the Lord is a God of justice. Blessed are all who wait for him!"

Isaiah 30:18 (NIV)

Translations

Key Words

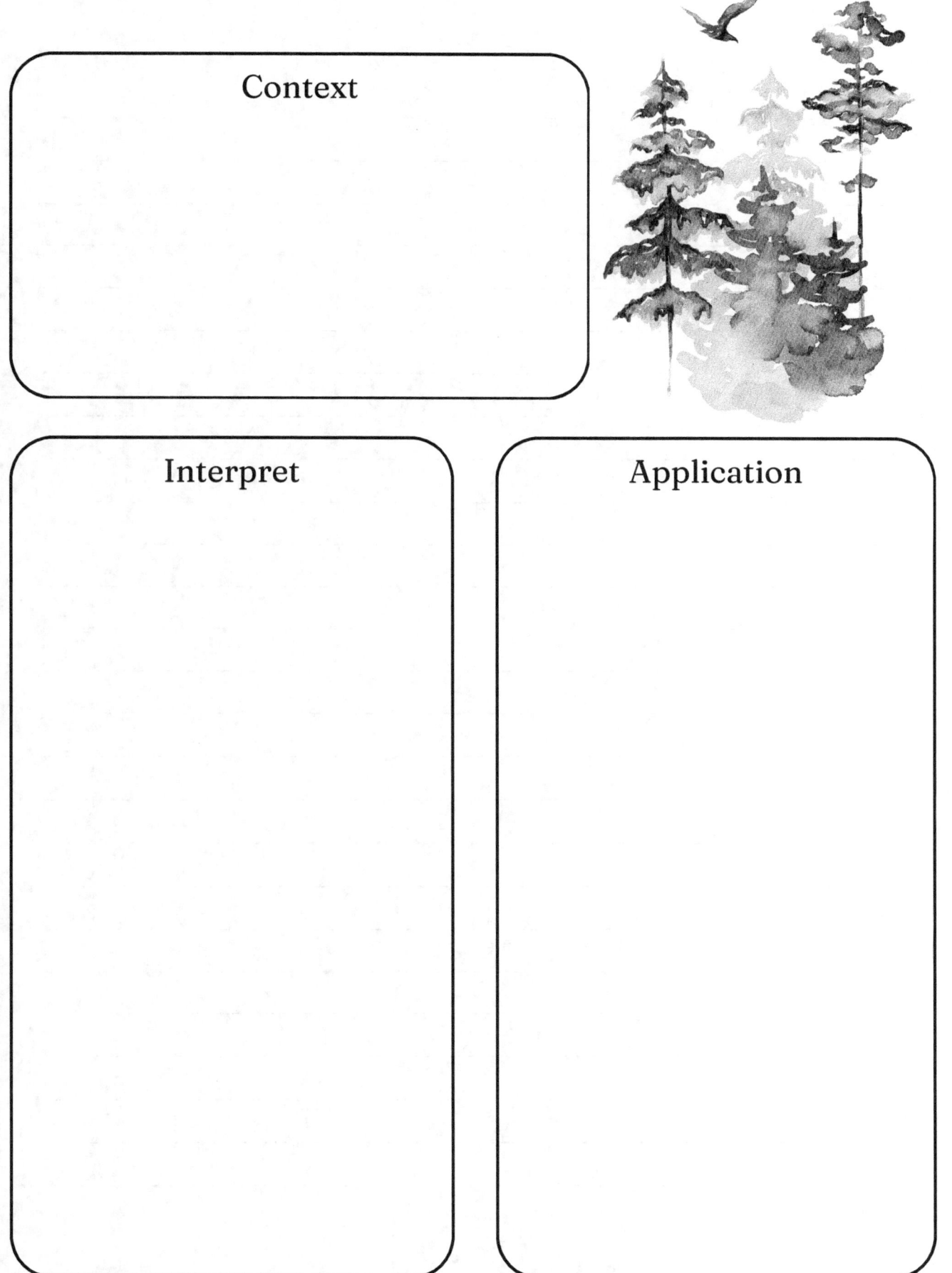

Context

Interpret

Application

not just another
prodigal story

Natalie Merrill

Reflection

What situation, possibly even from childhood, has brought confusion into your life?

_____

_____

_____

_____

_____

_____

_____

_____

_____

_____

_____

_____

_____

_____

_____

_____

_____

_____

_____

Can you think of some generational sins that have been passed down through your family?

_____

_____

_____

_____

_____

_____

_____

_____

_____

_____

_____

_____

_____

_____

_____

_____

_____

_____

_____

_____

_____

What sins are you holding onto? Will you repent and allow God's forgiveness to pour over you today?

_____

_____

_____

_____

_____

_____

_____

_____

_____

_____

_____

_____

_____

_____

_____

_____

_____

_____

_____

deepening your walk

Scripture Verse

"For we are God's masterpiece. He has created us anew in Christ Jesus, so we can do the good things he planned for us long ago."

Ephesians 2:10 (NLT)

Translations

Key Words

Context

Interpret

Application

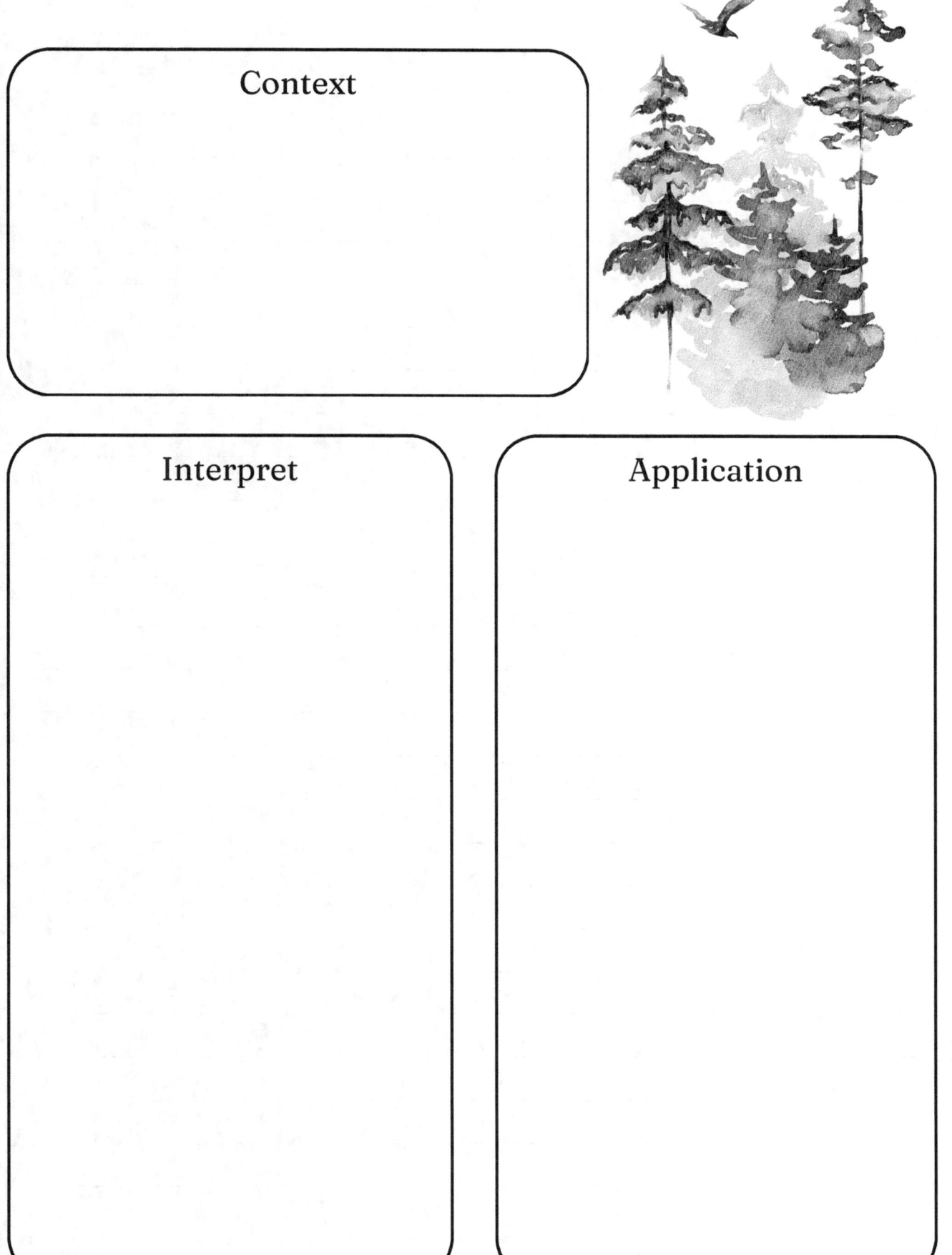

redemption story

Tina Jacobson

Reflection

What burdens from my past am I still carrying, and how are they affecting my ability to step into healing and freedom?

_____

_____

_____

_____

_____

_____

_____

_____

_____

_____

_____

_____

_____

_____

_____

_____

_____

_____

_____

If I fully believed that God sees me, loves me, and calls me worthy, how would my life begin to change?

_____

_____

_____

_____

_____

_____

_____

_____

_____

_____

_____

_____

_____

_____

_____

_____

_____

_____

_____

What is one step I can take today to release my past and embrace the healing and freedom God is offering me?

_____

_____

_____

_____

_____

_____

_____

_____

_____

_____

_____

_____

_____

_____

_____

_____

_____

_____

_____

deepening your walk

Scripture Verse

"Jesus answered, 'Everyone who drinks this water will be thirsty again, but whoever drinks the water I give them will never thirst. Indeed, the water I give them will become in them a spring of water welling up to eternal life.'"

John 4:12-13 (NIV)

Translations

Key Words

Context

Interpret

Application

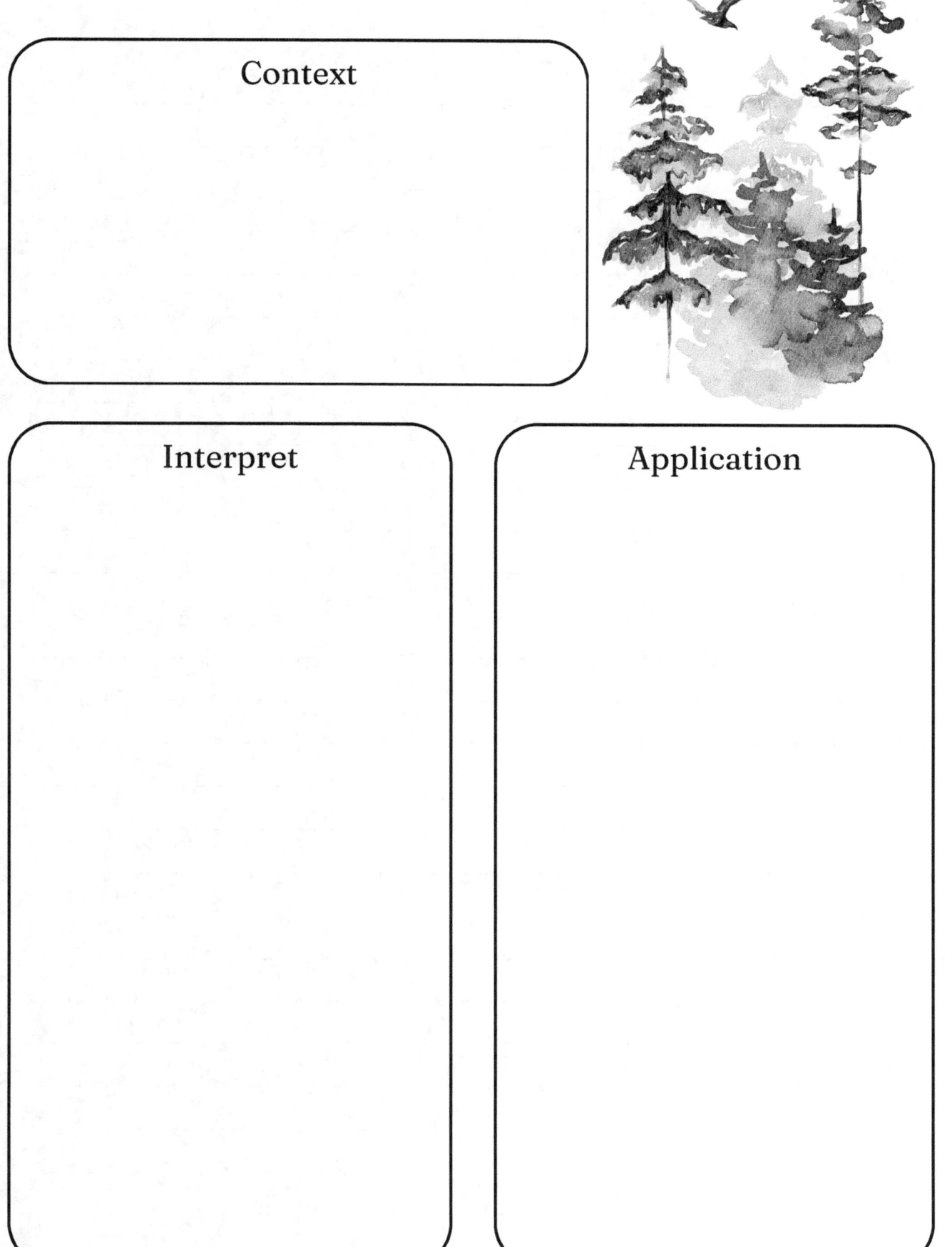

seasons of grace

Mantequilla Green

Reflection

How has my life changed since my loss?

_____

_____

_____

_____

_____

_____

_____

_____

_____

_____

_____

_____

_____

_____

_____

_____

_____

_____

_____

_____

_____

What unexpected emotions have surfaced during my grief?

How am I treating myself during the grieving process?

How am I different now compared to before the loss?

What new lessons have I learned about God during this time of grief?

_____

_____

_____

_____

_____

_____

_____

_____

_____

_____

_____

_____

_____

_____

_____

_____

_____

_____

_____

deepening your walk

Scripture Verse

"So they will fear the name of the Lord from the west
And His glory from the rising of the sun.
For He will come in like a narrow, rushing stream
Which the breath of the Lord drives [overwhelming the enemy]."
Isaiah 59:19 (AMP)

Translations

Key Words

Context

Interpret

Application

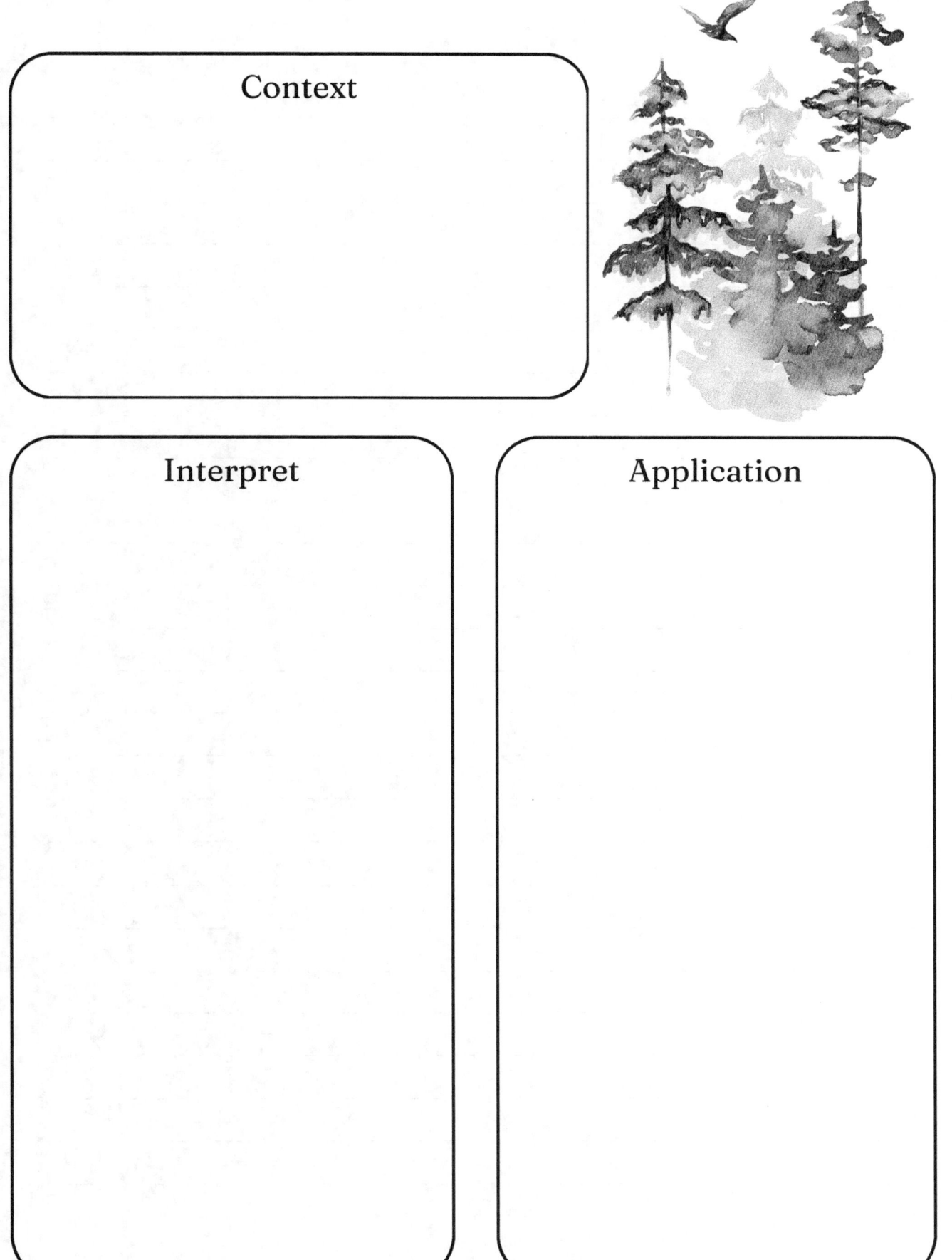

finding your god-given purpose through the storms of life

Crystal Duncan-Hogue

Reflection

How did you respond during your storms of life? What actions did you take?

_____

_____

_____

_____

_____

_____

_____

_____

_____

_____

_____

_____

_____

_____

_____

_____

_____

_____

_____

_____

Are you seeking God through daily devotion, prayer, worship and scripture?

_____

_____

_____

_____

_____

_____

_____

_____

_____

_____

_____

_____

_____

_____

_____

_____

_____

_____

_____

_____

_____

What are your next steps in discovering your God-given purpose?

_____

_____

_____

_____

_____

_____

_____

_____

_____

_____

_____

_____

_____

_____

_____

_____

_____

_____

_____

_____

deepening your walk

Scripture Verse

"'For I know the plans that I have for you,' declares the Lord, 'plans for prosperity and not for disaster, to give you a future and a hope.'"

Jeremiah 29:11 (NASB)

Translations

Key Words

Context

Interpret

Application

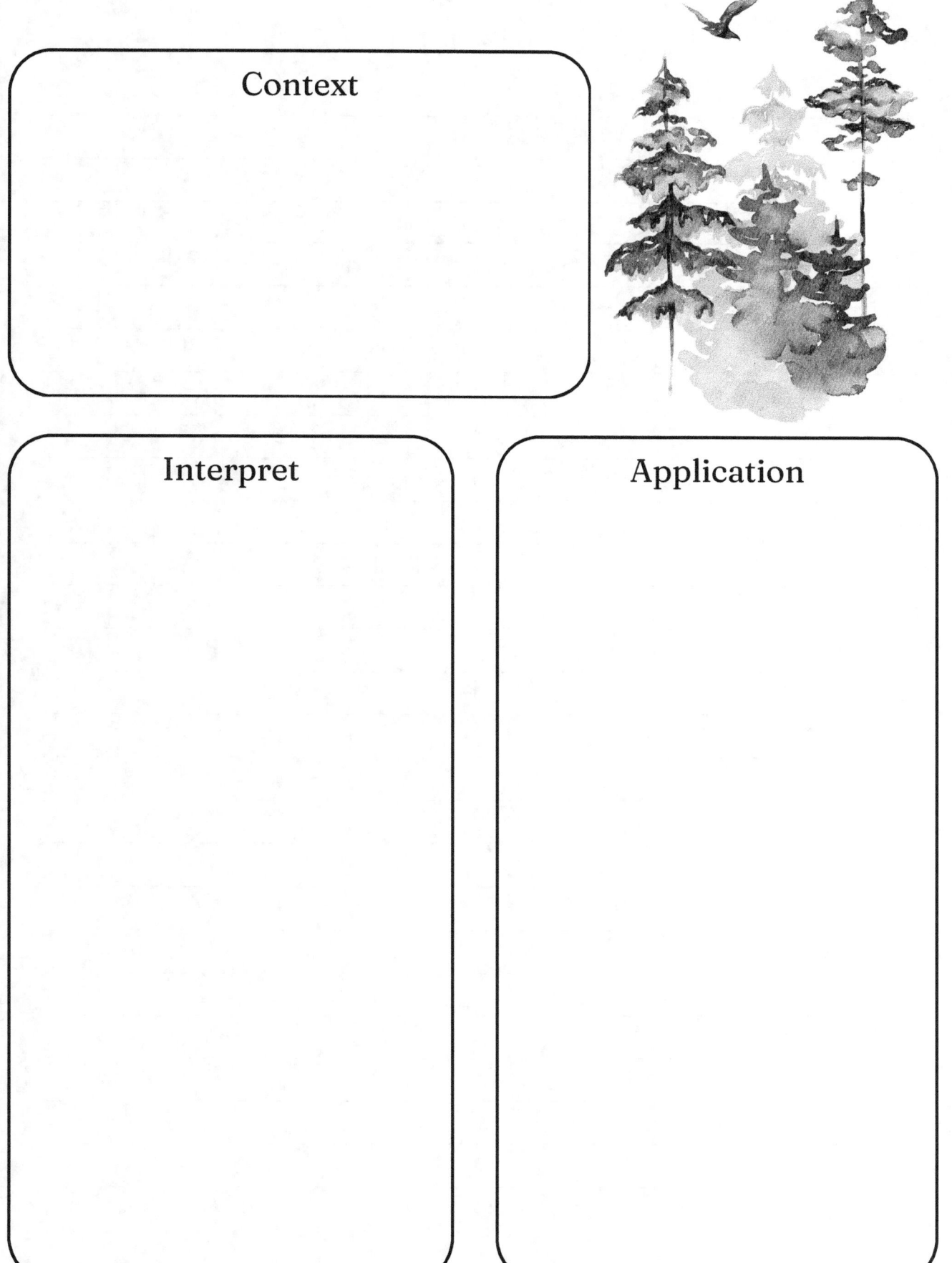

crossroads in life

A Journey of Decisions, Challenges, and Faith

Francisca Etuokwu-Benyeogor

Reflection

DECREE

I rise from every shackle and limitation that has held me down in Jesus name. I take judicial authority, rendering the plans of the enemy useless. I stand on God's great promises.

I may stand at the crossroads, but I am not lost. I decree that divine wisdom and clarity guide my steps. The path before me is illuminated with God's truth, and I will not be led by fear or confusion. Every decision I make aligns with God's perfect will, and no weapon formed against my destiny shall prosper.

_____

_____

_____

_____

_____

_____

_____

_____

_____

_____

_____

DECLARATION

I declare that I am stepping forward with boldness and confidence! I am equipped, empowered, and strengthened for the road ahead. The Lord is my shepherd, and He leads me in the way I should go. I declare that confusion has no power over me. My mind is clear, my spirit is steadfast, and my heart is anchored in faith. The Lord has not given me a spirit of fear but of love and sound mind! I trust that every choice I make is divinely ordered, and I will not be shaken. God walks with me, His voice directs me, and His presence surrounds me. My future is secure, my purpose is unfolding, and my breakthrough is near!

_____

_____

_____

_____

_____

_____

_____

_____

_____

_____

_____

_____

_____

_____

_____

_____

deepening your walk

Scripture Verse

"Blessed is the man whose strength is in You, whose heart is set on pilgrimage. As they pass through the Valley of Baca, they make it a spring; the rain also covers it with pools. They go from strength to strength; each one appears before God in Zion."

Psalm 84:5-7 (NIV)

Translations

Key Words

Context

Interpret

Application

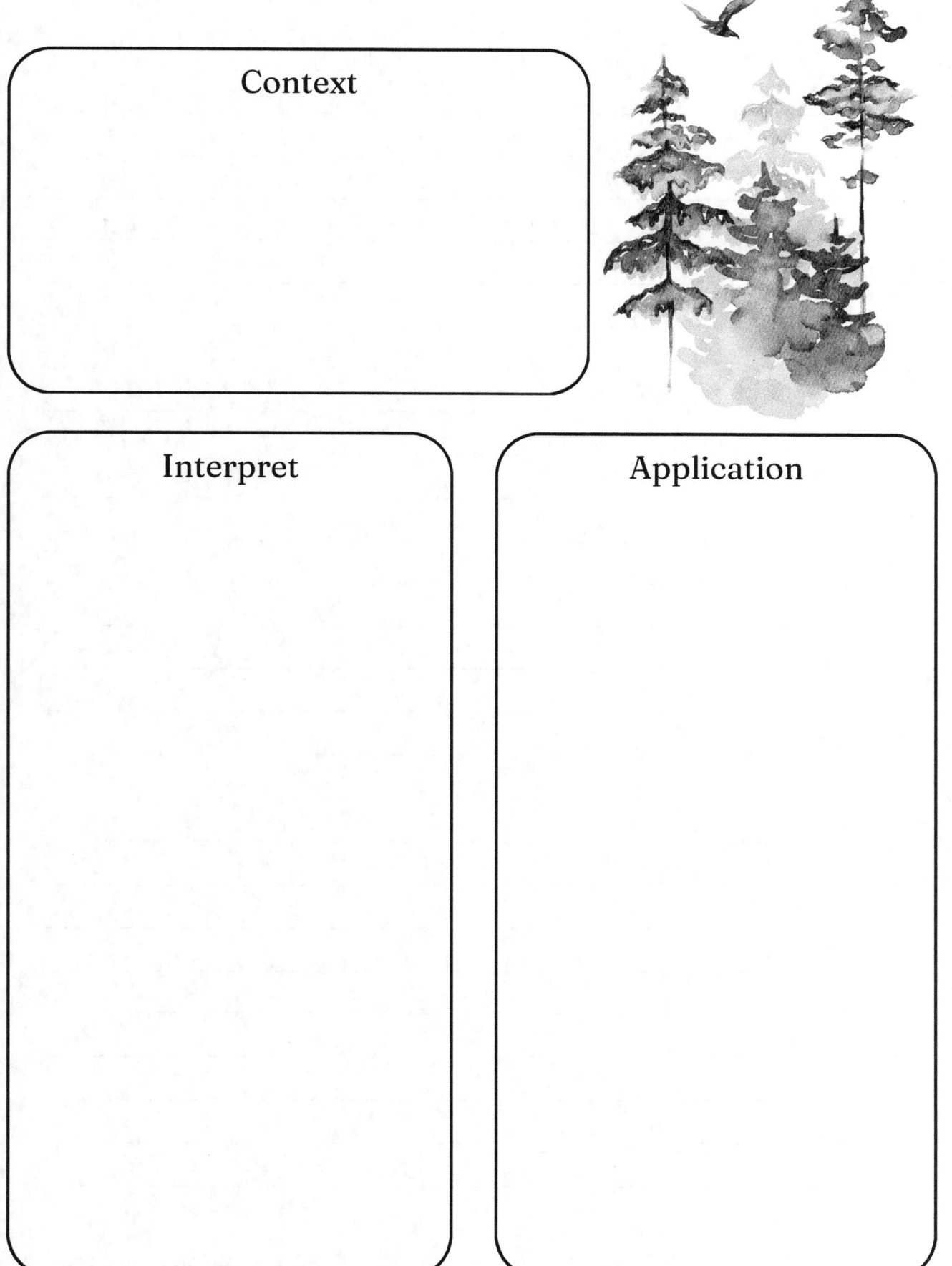

your call

Lori L. Dixon, Ed.S.

Dear *Elevating Wisdom on the Walk* Reader,

In these days we are living, you have witnessed greater revival than in past days. As you know, we are having powerful challenges and traumas, but we have a God who loves us through it all and in each step we take. Thank you for choosing to read this book and hear the stories of six women who believed and answered the Lord's calling to write for YOU.

You have read the deep stories of faith, loss, joy, healing, surrender, and transformation in the pages of this book. Many of the stories you have read from our women include their testimony of faith, too.

Which ones have touched your heart? Which one caused you to hear the Holy Spirit speaking to you? Which one aligned with your life circumstance now or even before?

You may be asking, "How do I give my life to Christ and what does that mean?" Are you feeling the nudging of the Holy Spirit to accept Christ into your life and into your heart? There is no age, time, place or certain words to say in this interaction with the Lord. It all begins with a simple understanding and a prayer of acceptance and surrendering of your life to Him. You receive the ability to see clearer the wisdom God gave you back in the Garden of Eden and to begin communing with Him again. You also open the door to letting Christ into your heart where He will never leave. He lives inside of us and walks with us every day.

Declaration

Begin by saying something like, "I believe in God the Father and in Jesus Christ, His Son. I am ready to begin a walk of faith today. I am inviting Christ into my heart."

> For everyone who calls on the name of the Lord will be saved.
>
> Romans 10:13 (TPT)

Prayer of Surrender

Using this as a guide, pray with a sincere heart:

Dear Father God, I come before You today with a heart filled with faith and love. I surrender my life—all of it, to You. I believe Jesus Christ was born free of sin, died on the cross for me and my sins, and rose from the grave three days later, I believe in Your beautiful gift of salvation, grace, and eternal life because of the sacrifice of Jesus Christ.

Lord, today I repent and turn from my old life. Your grace and mercy bring me to begin walking with a childlike faith. Today, in this moment, I ask you for a new life in which Jesus Christ and the Holy Spirit are within me. Thank you, God, for forgiving me and wiping away my sin away to become brand new in You.

In Jesus' Holy and precious name, Amen.

There is so much I want to share with you about this new walk of faith and how YOU become a sister or brother in the family of God. We are His children.

Will you choose to be a part of the family? We can't wait to greet you and walk with you. You may choose to reach out to one of the authors or to one of us in the WoW Team. We would also love for you to join our Facebook community called, "Wisdom on the Walk Author community" and share your testimony with us. We also have events and prayer team zoom calls together as a community of Christian women.

Being with others on this journey is important.

I suggest a few that I love below. Then, begin reading the scriptures shared with you in each of the chapters. Open your heart and let God speak truth into your life… today.

You may want to reach out and obtain the new "Deepening the Walk" journal and scripture mapping complimentary PDF. It is also available for a print copy on Amazon.

- **King James Version (KJV):** Great for memorizing verses
- **New International Version (NIV):** Easier to read in everyday language
- **The Passion Translation (TPT):** My favorite for connection to your life and sharing with others; only in New Testament, Proverbs, and Psalms at this time, with smaller books just for the Old Testament

If you prayed this prayer and asked Christ into your heart, please reach out to us. We want to pray for you and invite you to join us in our retreats, prayer team, bible studies, and more.

meet the authors

niki banning

NIKI BANNING is a Jesus-loving wife, mom, and Yaya.

She is a certified CORE Coach, and has been blessed to see her business, *NikiB Virtual Services*, blossom since starting in 2020. She has found a reignited passion for writing and editing, which led to Niki becoming a published author and launching *Story Guardian Editing Services*.

Through involvement first as a Caregiver and then as a leader for Stephen Ministry, Niki found her passion and calling: to come alongside others in support, and uplift them in business and life. But more importantly, she loves to encourage others in their personal relationship with God.

Niki is a relationship-builder, advocate, and ally. She has the ability to help others calm the chaos of their business and be a trusted partner and right hand. You can find Niki in her office, usually wearing fuzzy socks and accompanied by her also fuzzy office dog, Ruby.

nikibvirtualservices.com

Facebook: @nikibanning and @nikibvirtualservices

Instagram: @nikibanning

natalie merrill

NATALIE MERRILL is an author with a tender heart for prodigals. She is blessed to be the Director of Small Groups for *Alive at Last*, a non-profit organization working with traumatized, trafficked, and domestically abused women.

Natalie's most cherished title and job description is that of Mommy. Natalie's husband loves to describe her as sincere, fiercely loyal, caring, and compassionate.

Natalie enjoys social dancing and keeping fit. She has an associate degree in marketing, and enjoys being able to use her God-given creativity when she can.

Most of all, Natalie loves fellowship with brothers and sisters in Christ through Bible studies and everyday encounters. One of her favorite sayings is, "I love it when we all shine together!"

Join Natalie and learn how she found the depth of Jesus' compassionate grace through her own prodigal journey. You can connect with Natalie at authornataliemerrill@gmail.com.

tina jacobson

TINA JACOBSON is an author, speaker, and the visionary founder of Version of You by Tina. As a business and personal growth coach, she helps business owners and management teams unleash their full potential to become impactful leaders and mentors.

With extensive experience in Human Resources, business development, and management, Tina brings over 25 years of experience to support individuals and teams in achieving success.

In addition to coaching, Tina is proud to be a mom of one and Nonna to two beautiful grandchildren. As a health and personal growth mentor, Tina is dedicated to helping people live and lead with purpose, and find the very best version of themselves.

You can connect with Tina at *versionofyoubytina.com.*

mantequilla green

MANTEQUILLA GREEN is a best-selling author. She was featured in *Embracing Wisdom on the Walk*, which was released in April 2024.

As an educator of 25 years, Mantequilla has served in a myriad of roles, including teaching, mentoring, and leadership within the public school system. Presently, she serves as an administrator at a middle school in Austin, Texas. Mantequilla is an inspiration to her students and peers, and is a past recipient of the highly respected Teacher of the Year award.

Along with being a doctoral candidate, she also holds a Master's in Education and two Bachelor's degrees in Psychology and Communications (Journalism).

In her spare time, Mantequilla enjoys cooking, traveling, reading, and attending her local church. She can be reached at mshaleighgreen@hotmail.com.

crystal duncan-hogue

CRYSTAL DUNCAN-HOGUE is the Founder and CEO of CHM Bible Theatre, a nonprofit organization that fosters faith-based arts, theater, and leadership programs. Her mission is to orchestrate innovative and inspirational Bible stage plays for communities, enriched by culturally sensitive educational youth programming.

Crystal is a speaker, author, and an executive coach for Crystal Clear Coaching, helping other leaders of nonprofits. She is a playwright, artistic director, singer, songwriter, and wears many hats as a leader, wife, and mother. Crystal has cultivated meaningful connections across diverse spheres of the community, receiving several awards for community impact.

Crystal holds a bachelor's degree in theology and a master's degree in business administration. She also holds teaching and ministerial licenses. Driven by unwavering commitment, Crystal directs her multifaceted talents towards positively impacting society and encourages others to do the same.

She is happily married to Charles, a school principal. Together, they have raised three adult children. Her passion for life, the Bible, and serving others drives her leadership. Crystal aims to inspire unity, hope, and faith while fostering healing in communities.

You can find Crystal at:

www.chmbibletheatre.org

www.crystalclearcoach.org

Connect with Crystal at chmbtceo@gmail.com.

francisca etuokwu-benyeogor

FRANCISCA ETUOKWU-BENYEOGOR is is a Dallas resident, entrepreneur, Apostle, and founder of Armor of God Healing Ministries with the mission and vision to help, heal, and restore hope. Her Kingdom mandate is to impact lives globally with the transforming Word of God.

Francisca is author of an award-winning book, *The Waiting Game: When God Stops the Clock*. She is a transformational mental health coach and producer of Just One Word Show, which helps others experience God's glory and figure out "One Word" that will help shape their lives. Francisca has been featured in productions such as *The Voyage Dallas* and *The Whole Woman* magazines. As a servant leader, Francisca is a woman of grace, impact, and purpose, transforming lives globally with *Just One Word* through multiple platforms and speaking engagements.

Francisca's love for the Lord is contagious. Her hobbies include art, writing, fashion, music, and love for people. However, her greatest desire is to fulfill her God-given purpose.

Learn more about Dr. Francisca and her ministries at www.aoghm.org and email her at authorfrancisca32@gmail.com.

Did you gain wisdom on your walk?
Order more copies to pour into others!

www.walkwithlori.com/wisdomonwalk

or scan this code with your phone:

Wisdom on the Walk (WoW) book series, academy, and community!

Spirit-filled, Christ-centered, God-directed Life Stories

Has God specifically chosen YOU to be part of a new project to bring forth God's purpose in our lives? YOU are invited to join us in the next book in the WoW book series, as we share stories in this meaningful way. It is more than a book; it is an interactive journey of reflection, creativity, learning, connecting, and embracing God's work to influence and impact others. Your story will be intertwined with the writing of best-selling Lori L. Dixon, designs to engage you in furthering your purpose, and areas to reflect on His word in your own life.

I love how God has designed the expansion with further books, an academy of learning and writing, and an online community for sisterhood. What a beautiful and meaningful way to further HIS Kingdom by creating circles of disciples for unique and powerful purposes. As you will experience, we have workshops, prayer team circles, retreats, partners in writing, and engage in time together, sharing information, stories, insights, support, faith, and growth moments.

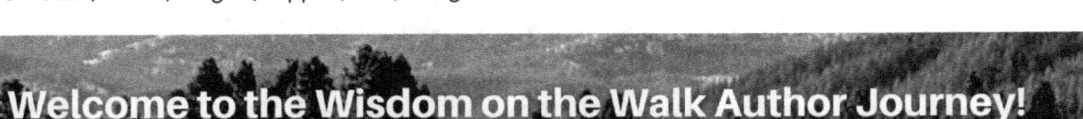

Welcome to the Wisdom on the Walk Author Journey!

Here are some quick items to know about the experience:

- We meet monthly for 9-12 months.
- Each session includes mentoring, learning, connection, interaction with other authors, bible study, and prayer. You will also have a 1:1 coaching session each month for guidance and direction in your writing, faith walk, social media presence, marketing, media, and more!
- Upcoming retreats in Dallas and beyond are planned for 2024 already.
- Further opportunities for sponsoring, speaking, and writing your own book are available.

Meet our LLD Legacy Publishing and Media Team:

Lori Dixon
owner, author, and your visionary leader in the process

Niki Banning
best-selling author, assistant, and leading editor

Callie Revell
publishing assistant, graphic design, and support

Do you hear that? A call to action. Are you feeling God is calling YOU? Have you ever thought He wants you to share your life story, healing, transformation, and insights with other women and glorify His work in YOU?

Your Story **is waiting to be told.**

Contact us for more information about the WoW Journey or to publish your book with us!

lld Legacy Publishing

meet Lori L. Dixon

@walkwithlori
@lorilanedixon

Lori L. Dixon, Ed.S. is a Visionary and Epiphany Expert with her business ventures, LLD Legacy Publishing, LLC, and Walk with Lori. Lori brings more than 4 decades of wisdom and experience working in education, therapies, business, and nonprofits. She is a best-selling author and publisher, theracoach, speaker, and a multiple international award-winning host and producer on TV. With her dynamic television appearances on Bravo's Real Housewives of Dallas, Lori understands the 'reality' of how the next chapter of life may be rewritten at any time. She may now be watched internationally on TV as a co-host on Lite It Up TV and Sawubona...I SEE You on ZondraTV Network on ROKU, AmazonFire, Chromecast, and iTunes.

Lori believes in finding the "heartstrings" in life, releasing the strongholds of fear, and living the life God has designed for you. As a writer for many years and a published author, editor, and frequent media influencer for others, Lori knew her passion would always be in the "stories" of our lives. She expanded her mission for writing and publishing with her own Christ-centered, faith-filled books, numerous compilations, and children's books. Lori believes we are all SEEN in our own God-given divine design and that we have a mission to share it right now within the world.

Through LLD Legacy Publishing, LLC, which is a full-service publishing company with editing, writing, illustrating, design, media, and marketing, she brings her passions together for each author. Her newest program, Wisdom on the Walk (WoW) is a unique experiential journey for women to become authors and further their own stories and missions for others.

VISIONARY LEADER

LORI L. DIXON, Ed.S.

Founder and Owner, LLD Legacy and Walk with Lori

TheraCoach, Publisher
International Multiple Award-Winning Host and Producer

469-855-0287
www.walkwithlori.com
lori@walkwithlori.com